LET'S DRAW STEP BY STEP

Let's Draw Things That Go

Kasia Dudziuk

WINDMILL
BOOKS

Published in 2017 by **Windmill Books,**
an Imprint of Rosen Publishing
29 East 21st Street, New York, NY 10010

Copyright © 2017 Arcturus Holdings Limited

Illustrations: Kasia Dudziuk
Text: JMS Books
Designer: Chris Bell
Editors: Joe Harris and Anna Brett

Cataloging-in-Publication Data

Names: Dudziuk, Kasia.
Title: Let's draw things that go / Kasia Dudziuk.
Description: New York : Windmill Books, 2017. | Series: Let's draw step by step | Includes index.
Identifiers: ISBN 9781499481853 (pbk.) | ISBN 9781499481860 (library bound) | ISBN 9781508192923 (6 pack)
Subjects: LCSH: Vehicles in art--Juvenile literature. | Drawing--Technique--Juvenile literature.
Classification: LCC NC825.V45 D83 2017 | DDC 743'.8962904--dc23

Manufactured in the United States of America
CPSIA Compliance Information: Batch #BW17PK: For Further Information contact Rosen Publishing, New York, New York at 1-800-237-9932

Contents

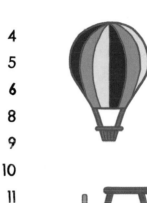

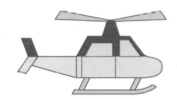

Can you draw a car?

1 Let's start with the car's wheels.

2 The body of the car comes next.

3 Now add the roof and windows.

4 Draw some lights on the front and back, and color it in. Don't forget the driver!

Try a hot air balloon.

1 It's just a simple circle to start.

2 Add the ropes...

3 ...and a basket for the passengers.

4 Hot air balloons are brightly colored!

Learn to draw a train.

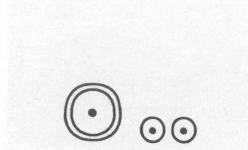

1 First draw the train's wheels – one big and two small.

2 Add a rectangle shape for the main body of the engine.

3 Draw a cab where the driver will sit and a light at the front.

4 Don't forget details like the smokestack and cab roof, and the grill in front of the wheels.

The train will need some train cars...

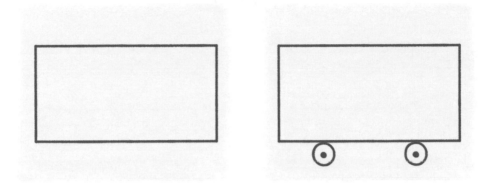

1 Start by drawing a rectangular shape.

2 Add some little wheels at the bottom.

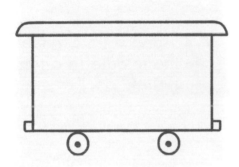

3 The train car needs a roof...

4 ...and some windows. Color it in.

Trains have different sorts of train cars.

A car for a circus train.

A coal tender.

Let's draw a bicycle.

1 The bicycle has two big wheels...

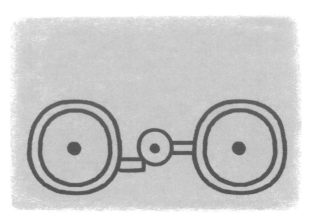

2 ...and a little wheel in the middle to attach the pedals.

3 Now draw the frame of the bicycle.

4 Add the handlebars, the seat and some spokes. Color your bicycle in bright shades.

Try drawing a jet plane.

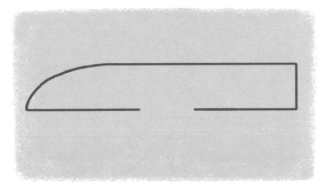

1 Draw a long shape for the body of the plane. Leave a gap at the bottom.

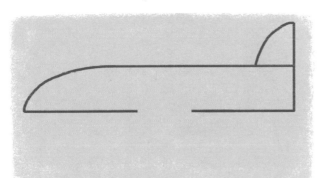

2 Don't forget to add a tail fin at the back...

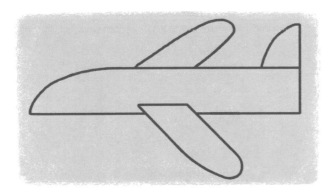

3 ...and two big wings on the sides!

4 Draw the windows and color your plane in.

Can you draw a rocket?

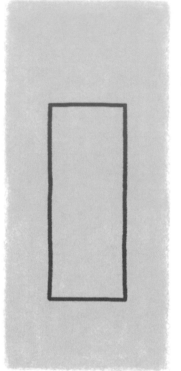

1 Start by drawing a rectangle.

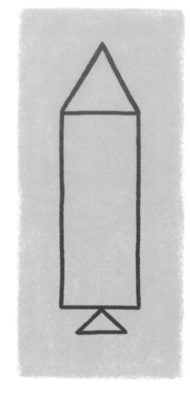

2 Add two triangles, one at the top and one at the bottom.

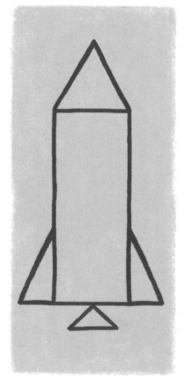

3 Now draw the side fins of the rocket.

4 Color it in – don't forget to add the windows and some flames at the bottom as the rocket takes off!

Now try a moon buggy.

1 Start by drawing two wheels.

2 Now add the base and the wheel arches.

3 The astronaut needs a seat and a control panel.

4 Color in the buggy – don't forget to add the satellite dish!

How about a motorbike?

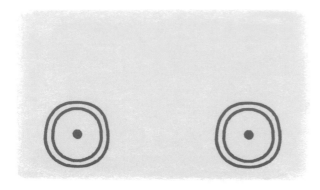

1 Start with two wheels. The tires are quite thin.

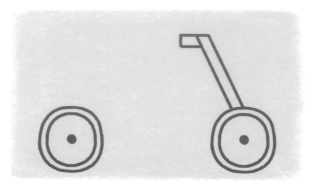

2 Add the front panel and the handlebars.

3 Now add the main body of the motorbike.

4 Draw a soft seat and some lights. Don't forget the footrest.

This motorbike has a sidecar for a passenger!

Try a fast speedboat!

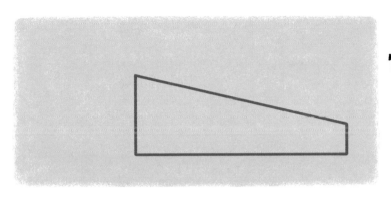

1 First draw this shape for the main part of boat.

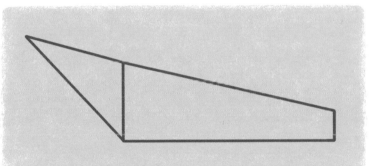

2 Add a triangle at the front.

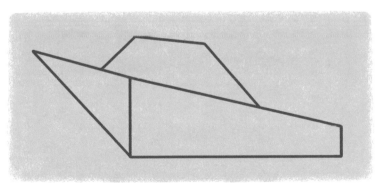

3 The speedboat needs a cabin!

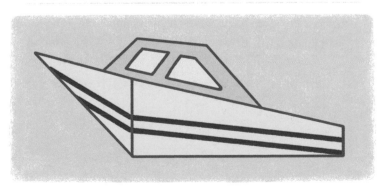

4 Draw the windows. Color the boat yellow and add some stripes.

Let's draw a seaplane.

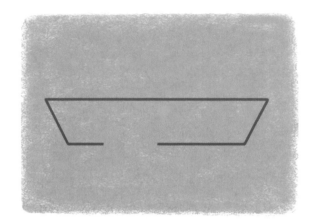

1 Start with the body of the seaplane. Leave a gap at the bottom.

2 Add a wing and the front strut.

3 Now draw the cabin and the float under the plane.

4 Add some windows, the tail fin and propeller, before coloring it in.

How about a hovercraft?

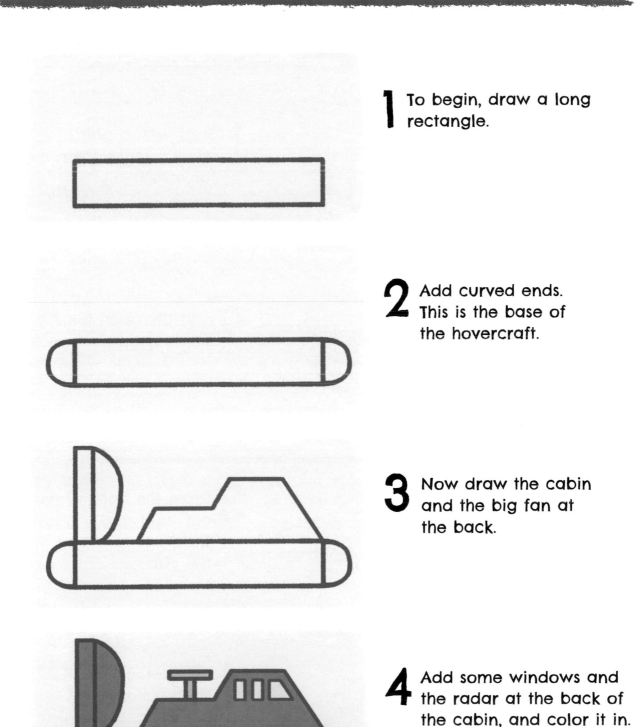

1 To begin, draw a long rectangle.

2 Add curved ends. This is the base of the hovercraft.

3 Now draw the cabin and the big fan at the back.

4 Add some windows and the radar at the back of the cabin, and color it in.

Draw a speedy sports car.

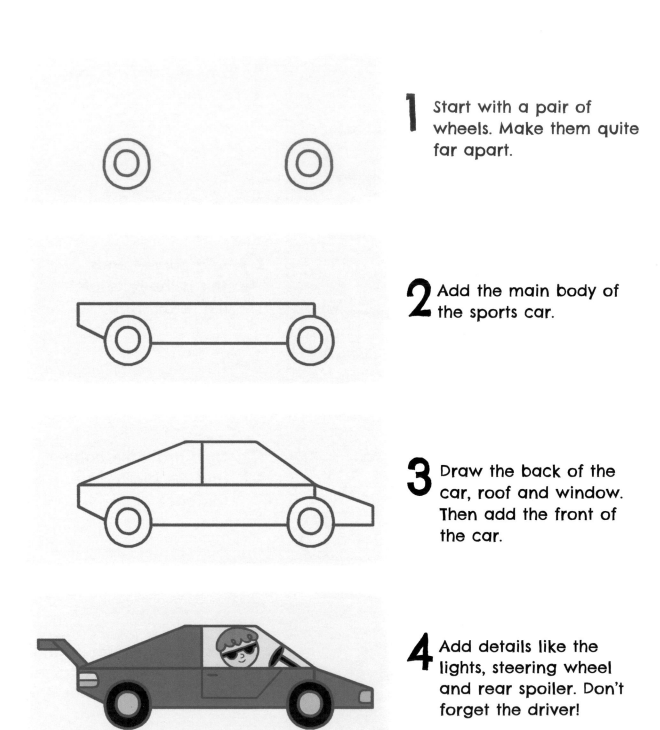

1 Start with a pair of wheels. Make them quite far apart.

2 Add the main body of the sports car.

3 Draw the back of the car, roof and window. Then add the front of the car.

4 Add details like the lights, steering wheel and rear spoiler. Don't forget the driver!

Can you draw lots of different sports cars?

Color one car red
to look like a Ferrari.

Remove the roof to
make another car
a convertible.

Some sports cars have
doors that open upwards
rather than outwards!

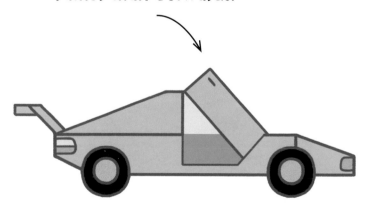

Beep-beep!

Draw a sailboat.

1 Draw this shape for the boat.

2 It needs a tall mast!

3 Add triangles for the sails.

4 Put a flag on top of the mast and add some portholes.

Now draw a fire truck.

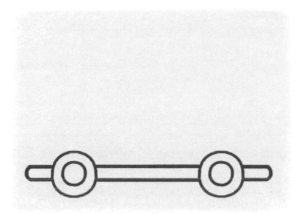

1 Begin with the base and two wheels.

2 Draw the cab at the front and a line at the back.

3 Add the light on the top and some windows. Draw the sides of the ladder.

4 Finish the ladder and add some lights to the front and back. Then draw the storage for the fire hose.

Can you add a firefighter driving the truck?

Let's draw a police car.

1 Start by drawing two wheels.

2 Draw two rectangles for the body of the car.

3 Add the roof of the police car with the flashing light on top.

4 Draw some windows and a steering wheel, and add some lights to the front and back.

Now try an ambulance.

1 Start by drawing two circles for the wheels.

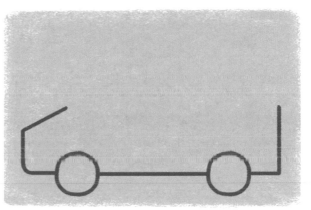

2 Now draw this shape for the bottom of the vehicle.

3 Add the cab at the front with a window, and complete the roof. Draw a stripe along the side.

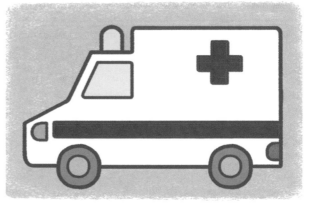

4 Add the lights and the red cross. Don't forget to color the stripe too.

Try drawing a lifeboat.

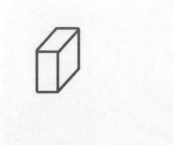

1 Begin with a box shape like this.

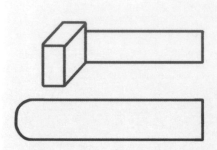

2 Draw two more shapes like this to form the sides of the boat.

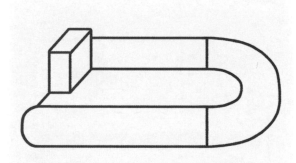

3 Add a rounded shape for the front of the boat and finish the back.

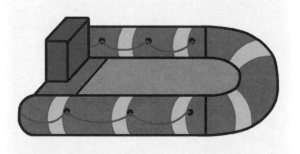

4 Draw stripes around the sides, add a rope to each side and color your lifeboat in.

How about a helicopter?

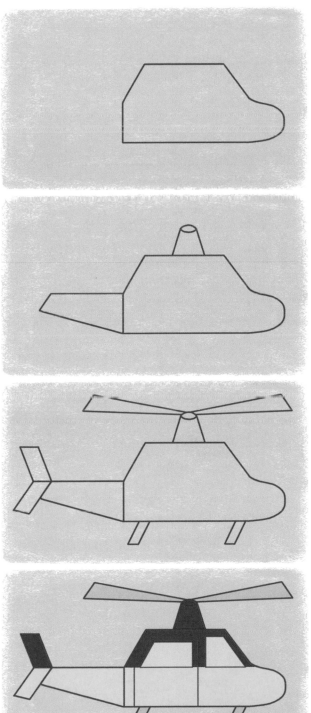

1 Start your helicopter by drawing this shape for the cockpit.

2 Add the tail of the helicopter and a cone shape on the top.

3 Draw the rotor blades at the top, the fins at the back and two struts at the bottom.

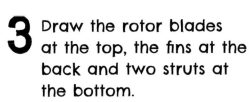

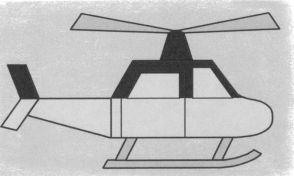

4 Finish by adding a door, windows and a landing skid. Then color it in.

Draw a pickup truck.

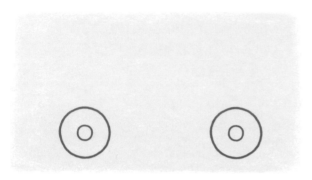

1 Begin by drawing two wheels. The tires are quite thick.

2 Add some straight lines like these to form the body.

3 Draw the bumpers and the cab of the truck.

4 Finish by adding a window, a door handle and some lights, before coloring it in.

Who is driving your truck?

24

Now try a snowplow.

1 Start by drawing two wheels, just like the pickup truck.

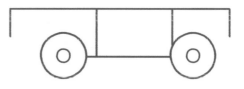

2 Add some straight lines like these to form the body.

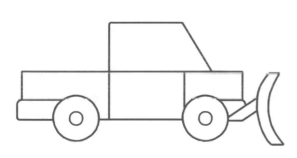

3 Draw the bumpers and cab. Then add the plow at the front of the truck.

4 Add a window and door, and lights at the front and back. Finish by drawing a flashing light on top.

Draw some snow and a snowman!

Learn to draw a Jet Ski.

1 Let's start with the bottom of the Jet Ski.

2 The front comes next.

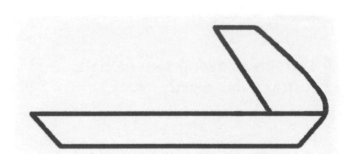

3 Now add a side panel.

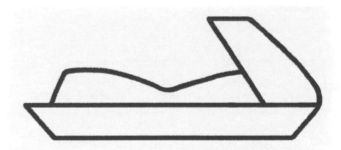

4 Draw the steering handle and the seat. Now you can color it in.

Can you draw a Jet Ski pulling the water-skier?

Let's try a submarine!

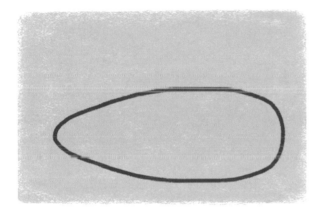

1 Start by drawing this shape for the submarine body.

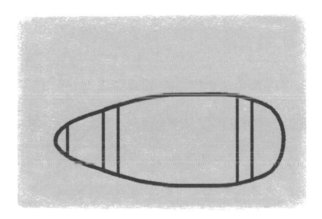

2 Draw some straight lines down the body like this.

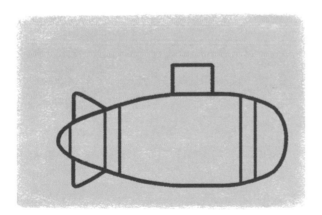

3 Add a square tower at the top and fins at the back.

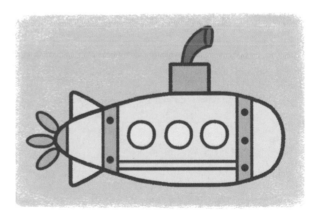

4 Draw the rear propeller and some portholes. Don't forget the periscope!

What about a sleigh?

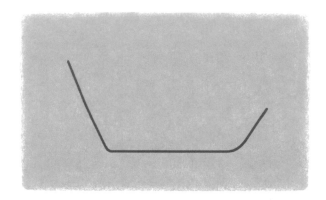

1 First draw three straight lines like this.

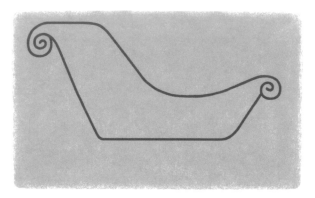

2 Then draw a curly line across the top.

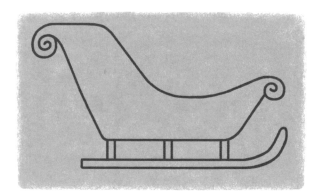

3 Add the runner at the bottom of the sleigh.

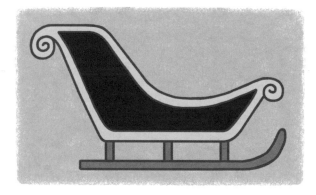

4 Color the sleigh red and gold, and the runner brown.

Can you draw a reindeer to pull the sleigh?

Now draw a tractor.

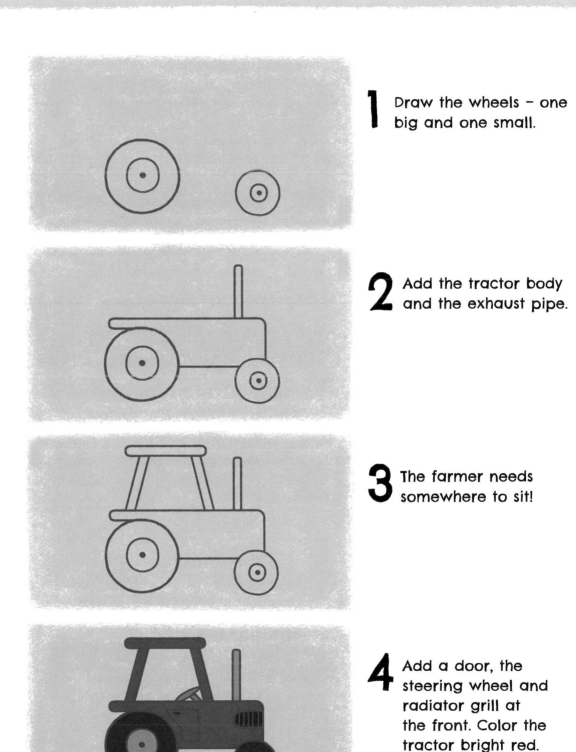

1 Draw the wheels – one big and one small.

2 Add the tractor body and the exhaust pipe.

3 The farmer needs somewhere to sit!

4 Add a door, the steering wheel and radiator grill at the front. Color the tractor bright red.

Glossary

hovercraft A vehicle that travels on a cushion of air just above the water or land.

landing skid The part that supports the helicopter when it lands.

periscope An instrument with lenses and mirrors that allows people to see over the top of things such as water.

porthole A window on a boat.

propeller Metal blades that spin around to make a boat or plane move forward and back.

radar A device for detecting and tracking faraway objects.

radiator A part of a vehicle that helps keep the engine cool.

rotor blades The long blades that spin to keep a helicopter in the air.

sidecar A small cab attached to the side of a motorcycle for a passenger.

smokestack A chimney on a train for carrying smoke away.

spoiler The part on the rear of the car that helps keep it steady when it goes very fast.

tender A train car for carrying fuel or water attached to a steam train.

Further reading

1000 Things to Draw by Kirsteen Robson (Usborne Publishing Ltd, 2015)

How to Draw 101 Things that Go by Nat Lambert (Top That Publishing, 2012)

I Can Draw Planes, Trains & Moving Machines by Philippe Legendre (Walter Foster, 2014)

Junior How to Draw Cars, Trucks and Planes by Kate Thompson (Top That Publishing, 2011)

Learn To Draw Things that Go! (Peter Pauper Press, 2014)

Websites

For web resources related to the subject of this book, go to: **www.windmillbooks.com/weblinks** and select this book's title.

Index